The hillfort of Little Solsbury where the Iron Age inhabitants of the Bath region settled before the Roman invasion.

In the beginning

The springs of Bath are very ancient, first used by groups of hunters 7000 years ago. In the centuries before the Romans came the Celtic inhabitants revered the springs as sacred to the goddess Sulis.

The hot mineral water gushing out of the overflow in the reservoir wall.

Coins of the Celtic tribe – the Dobunni. They were found in the Sacred Spring.

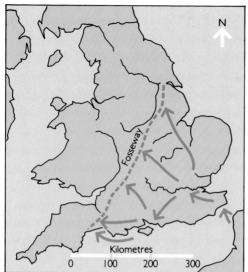

Path of the Roman conquest.

The Romans Arrive

The Roman army landed in Kent in AD 43 to begin its systematic conquest of Britain. After overcoming initial tough resistance, the legions fanned out across the south-east of the country with the intention of creating a frontier zone separating the fertile lowlands from the more difficult terrain of Cornwall, Wales and Northern Britain.

The frontier, established between AD 43–7, ran from the south coast near Exeter to the Humber estuary. It was a military buffer zone 20–30 miles wide, through which passed lines of communication all well protected by forts. One essential component of the system was a single lateral road, now known as the Fosseway. It provided the means to move supplies or troops quickly in times of

Fosseway at Stratton-on-the-Fosse looking north.

trouble. Much of the Fosseway still survives as a modern road.

The Fosseway crossed the River Avon somewhere in the vicinity of Bath, probably to the west of the city. Another road, from London to the port of Sea Mills crossed both the river and the Fosseway north of the city, while a third from the Dorset coast, made for the same crossing point.

In all probability a fort, manned by an auxiliary garrison, guarded the crossing in the early years of the conquest. It has not yet been located but one possible site is on a well-drained patch of gravel just to the east of the major bridging point. Early imported samian pottery of the right date has been found here from time to time. Several military tombstones were recovered from the cemetery lining the Fosseway.

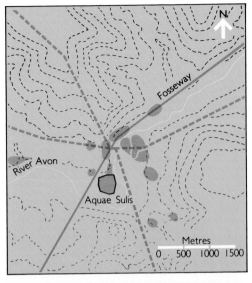

A strategic crossing marks the site of early Bath.

Tombstone of a Roman cavalryman Lucius Vitellius Tancinus from Spain. He died after 26 years of service aged 46 and was buried at Bath.

Bath today seen from the south-west.

The area around the three hot springs of Bath was very soon developed by the Romans, who would have been attracted by a Celtic shrine at the main (or King's Bath) spring. The ancient sacred location was taken over and the local deity, Sulis, was conflated with the Roman goddess Minerva. Some time in the 60s or 70s AD work began on a new stone-built temple complex which was to dominate the town for the next four centuries. As part of this building programme the spring was contained within a reservoir and used to supply a great thermal bathing establishment which grew up to the south of the temple. Another building which we might expect to find in a great religious

complex of this kind is a theatre for religious and secular performances. A likely position for it in Bath would be somewhere to the north of the temple, cut into the face of a steep natural slope known to exist at this point. No foundations have yet been found but several finely sculpted blocks, dug out from beneath Westgate Street last century, could well be part of it. One day further evidence may come to light.

Together the temples, baths and theatre would have formed the nucleus of the great religious complex – the temple of Sulis Minerva – from which the Roman settlement, Aquae Sulis, took its name. The two other, lesser, springs, the Cross Bath and Hot Bath

JOHN RONAYNE

springs, were also in existence in Roman times and both have produced Roman sculpture and inscriptions suggesting that they too may have been sacred shrines. One sculpture, from the Cross Bath, shows scenes from the legend of Aesculapius, the god of healing – highly appropriate to a healing spring.

Of the other buildings of Roman Bath we know very little but there is evidence to suggest that the area between the religious centre and the surrounding wall was packed with structures. In the south-west corner there was another bathing establishment, quite possibly curative baths associated with the Hot Bath spring. Elsewhere walls, hypocausts and mosaic floors of houses have been found indicating a high level of luxury enjoyed by those who lived around the temple.

The Roman walls of Bath, later rebuilt as the medieval city wall, enclosed all the principal buildings within an area of just under 10 hectares. This is very much smaller than Roman country towns like Winchester, Chichester and Silchester and suggests that the wall, rather than being a city wall may have been built as a *temenos* boundary defining the religious area. Building certainly spread outside the wall, particularly along the Fosseway to the north and this may have been the commercial zone growing up at the main cross roads and bridging point.

Reconstruction of the Roman city.

The Sacred Spring

The main spring in the centre of Bath – the King's Bath spring – bubbles out of the ground at the rate of a quarter of a million gallons a day, the water maintaining a consistent temperature of 46·5°C. The water we now see is ancient rain which fell, probably on the Mendips, about 10,000 years ago and penetrated deep into the earth where it was warmed by the natural heat of the earth's core. The hot and steaming spring must have been awe-inspiring to the Celts and Romans.

The Sacred Spring reconstructed.

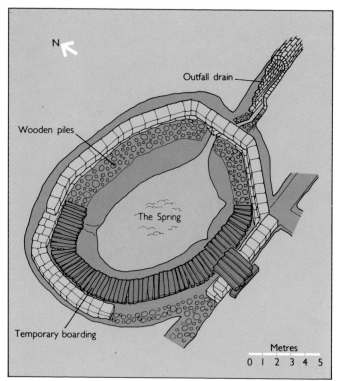

Controlling the Waters

In its natural state the spring would have bubbled up in a broad hollow filled with a thick deposit of black mud and sand, the water flowing away in a shallow valley to the River Avon. The area around the spring head was marshy and would have supported thick vegetation including alder and willow. How the Iron Age inhabitants treated the spring we are unlikely ever to know because the later Roman buildings have obscured so much, but in all probability the central pool was kept clear so that worshippers could approach the waters.

Ten or twenty years after the Roman armies conquered this part of Britain, skilled Roman engineers began to tame the flow. As the result of the 1979–80 excavation in the spring itself we can now build up an accurate picture of the way in which they went about this work. First of all it would have been necessary to create a solid working platform around the spring head. This they did by ramming hundreds of oak piles down into the mud to form a wide ring enclosing the

An early stage in the construction of the Roman reservoir.
Excavation in progress in the Sacred Spring in 1979.

spring. Planks laid across the tops of the piles formed a stable working platform. From this the construction work could begin.

One of the main concerns of the engineers was to lower the water-level so that the foundations of the reservoir wall could be built. To do this they must have dug an overflow canal to channel off the water, at the same time removing mud and sand from the spring head itself. A narrow gap in the ring of piles allowed the spring to be drained down to the level of the overflow channel.

It was at this stage that work began on the construction of the reservoir wall. First a foundation trench was dug around the outside of the piled platform, and in it more piles were rammed to form a solid base. On this the massive square blocks of stones of the reservoir wall were laid leaving a square hole 30 cm across for the spring water to pass through into the overflow channel. Gradually the reservoir wall was raised until it reached the desired height of about 2 metres, the only opening being a slot for a sluice set in the east wall.

The stone blocks of the reservoir wall were fitted tightly together without mortar but were held firm with iron clamps set in lead. When the wall was complete the entire inner face was lined with massive sheets of lead nearly a centimetre thick. The upper edge was folded back over the masonry while the lower edge was folded forwards across the tops of the piles which had been packed around with clay. The vertical joints between the sheets were melted together. In this way the engineers created a completely watertight lining but just to make sure of the lower edge a wide step of waterproof pink mortar was laid with large tiles set in its upper surface.

There were two reasons for creating such a massive reservoir. First, a head of water was required to feed the bathing establishment built to the south. Water still flows into the Great Bath through the original lead-lined channel from an opening in the very top of the reservoir. The second reason shows the particular skill of the Roman engineers. They must have observed that the spring constantly brought up quantities of black sand from deep in the earth. Clearly this sand would have clogged the plumbing system if some measures had not been taken to cope with it. By building a reservoir 2 metres deep

the engineers had, in fact, created a settling tank in which the unwanted sediment would remain. The water drawn off at the top was quite clear.

After a while, of course, the reservoir would begin to fill with sand. The engineers had expected this and had designed the sluice in the east wall specially for this purpose. When it was judged that the silt was deep enough, the sluice would be opened so that the force of the water could wash out the sediment into the main drain. The drain itself was built large enough for a man to be able to walk along to shovel away any obstruction that might have formed.

The reservoir was partly excavated in 1878 when most of the lead lining was ripped off and sold and a concrete roof, forming the floor of the King's Bath, was built. A hundred years later, it was necessary, for structural reasons, to remove the floor so that the south wall of the Pump Room could be underpinned. An archaeological excavation, in the depths of the reservoir, was mounted first and produced sufficient evidence for us to be able to unravel the complex but fascinating building process just described. The excavation also brought to light thousands of votive offerings thrown into the spring by Roman worshippers nearly 2000 years ago.

Detail of the construction of the reservoir wall.

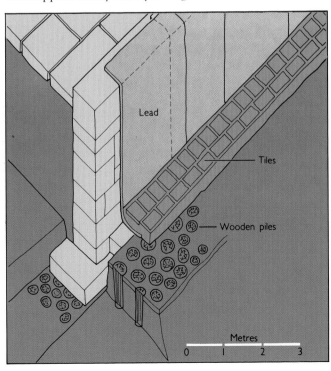

Lead

Tiles

Wooden piles

Metres

0   1   2   3

Offerings to the Gods

To the Romans, the spring was far more than just a source of hot water – it was a sacred place where mortals of this world could communicate with the deities of the underworld. People came in their thousands not only to see the remarkable phenomenon of the hot springs but to seek the assistance of the goddess Sulis Minerva.

To begin with the Sacred Spring was open to the sky and easy for all to approach either from the precinct of the temple or by means of three large window openings in the wall which divided the baths from the temple, two of which remain to this day. Later, towards the end of the second century, there was a major change in use when the reservoir was enclosed within a massive chamber roofed with a brick and concrete vault. Now (as our illustration on page 9 indicates), the spring became a dark and mysterious place available only to those who viewed it from the south through the three large window openings. The door in the north wall was too small for general use and was probably designed to allow the priest to approach the waters for ritual purposes. Another embellishment was the addition of decorative features, very probably statues, which stood on plinths just projecting from the water-level between a framing of columns. Nothing now remains of the statues but the impression they would have given on a cold winter day, appearing to float on the surface of the water with steam swirling around them, must have been awe-inspiring.

The excavation in the bottom of the spring 100 years ago and the recent excavation have together brought to light a remarkable collection of metal votive offerings thrown by worshippers into the waters. Most numerous were the coins of which more than 12,000 have now been recovered spanning the entire Roman period. The temptation to throw coins into the spring and to wish is a universal and timeless human reaction. For the Roman worshippers it may have been less casual that it is for us – perhaps it was necessary for them to make a cash thank-offering to the goddess for some service she might have rendered them. Most of the coins were fairly small denominations, but four of gold must each represent a particularly expensive act of piety.

The power of the deity

One of the uses to which the Sacred Spring was put was as a means of bringing retribution on an enemy. If someone had done you wrong, for example stolen your cloak, and you were not quite sure who it was, you would go to the temple scribe and ask him to help compose a message to the goddess. It would normally be in a standard form written in a kind of legal language – for example *"May he who stole my cloak, whether he be man or woman, boy or girl, freedman or slave, become impotent and die. It may have been ..."* and here you would provide a list of suspects. While the cause and the curse varied, the general formula was much the same.

By cursing in this way, even if you were not sure who the culprit was, the mere fact that his or her name was listed meant that the goddess, who would know, was called upon to act. It also meant that the person who had done the wrong would live in constant fear of having been cursed.

Once the message was composed it would be inscribed on a sheet of pewter either by the scribe or, as one text suggests, it might be copied out by the person issuing the curse. If this was the general rule it would make sense of the considerable variety of handwritings represented on the 90 or so curses found in the spring at Bath.

When ready, the curse would be thrown into the spring sometimes having first been rolled up. The Bath curses are remarkable documents reflecting not only the petty irritations of everyday life but providing long lists of the names of the inhabitants with details of their families and social status.

Coins, metal jugs and cups and pewter curses formed the bulk of the finds thrown into the spring but there were in addition a number of other, generally unique items.

Perhaps the most notable is a fine bronze penannular brooch with its terminals inset with red enamel, each representing a mythological scene: one depicts two birds, one behind the other, the other shows a crow pecking at a fish. The brooch must have been of considerable value and reflects on the piety of the donor.

Another rather unusual object is a semicircular block of ivory carved stylistically with what appears to be a pair of breasts. This is the only piece we have depicting the human body and is in interesting contrast to the sacred springs found in France where carvings, usually in wood, representing parts of the human body which the deity is expected to cure, are comparatively common. If the spring at Bath was believed to have had curative properties, which is quite likely because Minerva was endowed with powers of healing, then we can only suppose that the ritual was different from that of the French shrines, involving perhaps, the immersion of the whole body in the sacred waters in the great bath.

Another group of objects, found in the outfall drain 100 years ago but probably washed out of the spring by the force of the water, was a collection of 34 engraved gem stones. The records of the find are not good enough to make it clear if the gems were all found together (and if so were probably thrown in in a bag) or if they were scattered finds, but since none was found in the recent excavation in spite of the fact that all the sediment was finely sieved, it is more likely that the group had been thrown in all together. Perhaps they were the stock in trade of a gem-cutter or a collection of valued heirlooms – we will never know.

Together, then, the objects found in the spring and the drain show something of the aims, aspirations and the piety of the people who visited the Sacred Spring during the four hundred years or so of the Roman occupation. Much has been recovered from the excavations but a great deal more of the ritual deposit still remains to be excavated. It has been deliberately left for the future. Perhaps in another hundred years' time even more exciting discoveries will be made.

Penannular brooch of bronze with red enamel set in the terminals.

Gemstone engraved with a discus thrower, 12.5 by 10mm.

The Temple

The city of Aquae Sulis lay on the very fringes of the Roman world where old Celtic deities predominated, yet remarkably the temple of Sulis Minerva dominating the city was a purely classical conception.

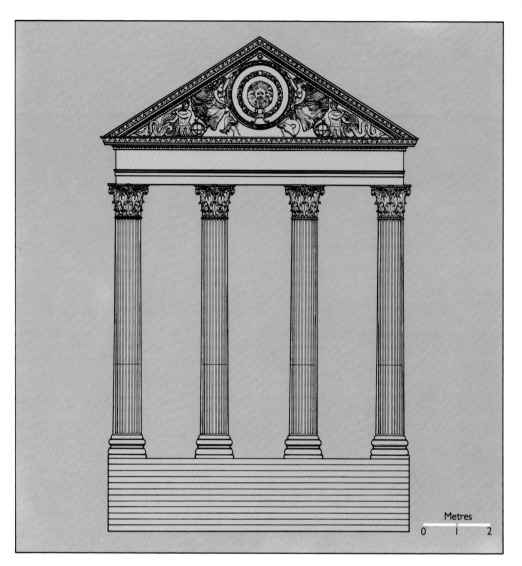

The east front pediment of the temple of Sulis Minerva.

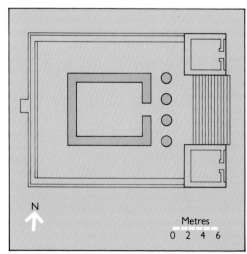

Plan of the temple of Sulis Minerva.

N

Metres
0 2 4 6

The original temple, built in the 60s or 70s of the first century AD, was a classical building consisting of a small cella (or cult room) fronted by a pronaos (porch) with four large Corinthian columns supporting a richly decorated pediment. The whole building was set high on a podium reached by steps.

At the end of the second century the early building was encased within a much larger structure. In front a new flight of steps was built between what appear to be two side chapels, each entered through a door set centrally between projecting pilasters. Behind the chapels and around the old temple was a raised platform or ambulatory, making the temple look far more like native temples found elsewhere in Britain.

The Gorgon's head pediment from the temple.

The great glory of the temple, then as now, is the decorated pediment, dominated by the fearsome Gorgon's head. It is a remarkable piece in many ways: its sculpture shows a vitality rare elsewhere in Britain while the subject matter is a confusion of Roman and Celtic ideas.

The design is very Roman – a Gorgon's head on a shield held aloft by two winged Victories – but when you look closely at the head it is not a classical Gorgon at all (always a female) but a male and a male who is carved in a very Celtic style with billowing moustaches, lentoid eyes and a heavy beetling brow.

What was in the minds of the craftsmen who designed and carved it we will never

know but perhaps in the Gorgon motif they saw the opportunity to create a centrepiece which incorporated the attributes of a male god of the waters (like the Roman Neptune) and also a sun god with flaming hair. Such a combination would be an appropriate symbol for the hot waters of Bath over which Sulis Minerva presided.

The links with the classical Minerva are rather clearer. The Gorgon's head shield itself is often associated with the goddess. Below the shield to the right is a small owl standing on a helmet, reminding us of Minerva's reputation for wisdom while to the left there is a Corinthian helmet with a high crest which reflects Minerva's more warlike attributes.

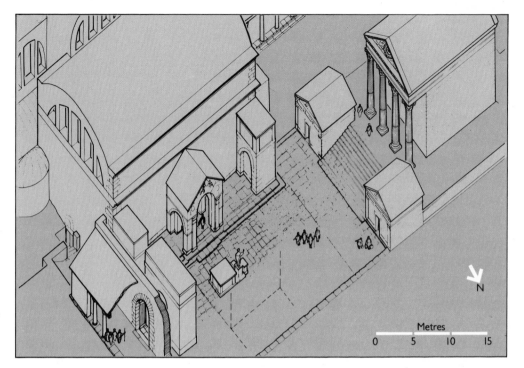

General view of the temple precinct in the fourth century

The Temple Precinct

A Roman temple was essentially a place where the cult statue of the deity and the sacred objects could be kept. All the religious ceremonies would have taken place in front, either on the temple steps or in the precinct around the altar where the congregation could gather out in the open. It is therefore totally unlike a Christian church where everything goes on inside the building.

In Bath we now know a great deal about the arrangement of the precinct largely as the result of the excavations of 1979–83 in the area beneath the Pump Room.

In its original state, towards the end of the first century AD, the temple stood in the western half of a large rectangular court enclosed by colonnaded walks. In front of it was the inner precinct, a rectangular area paved with massive slabs of lias limestone, and in the centre of this stood the altar. At this stage the Sacred Spring was completely open – a simple polygonal pool of steaming water surrounded by a low balustrade. The overall impression would have been of uncluttered spaciousness: the entire concept was purely classical.

Towards the end of the second century, or early in the third, the temple complex under-

went a far-reaching programme of renovation and change. The temple itself was enlarged, but more impressive was the enclosing of the Sacred Spring within a huge hall roofed with a masonry vault. The reason for this implies a change in ritual practice. That such an elaborate programme could be undertaken shows that the local community was flourishing unless, of course, the entire refurbishment was the result of a single benefaction from a wealthy patron.

The enclosing of the reservoir created problems, for its north wall had to be built across soft marshy ground and, in spite of its considerable foundations, it soon began to settle. The response of the Roman engineers was extremely clever. The north wall had to be buttressed but to do so could well have ruined the appearance of the precinct. What they did was to construct three massive buttresses, disguised as monumental architecture and bound visually together by appearing to be built on a single raised platform, or podium, running the length of the reservoir enclosure. The central of the three buttresses was designed as a four-way porch (quadrifrons) giving dignity to the way from the altar to the little doorway leading to the spring. The overall effect was greatly to increase the grandeur of the precinct.

The altar was the centrepiece of the temple complex because it was here that the temple officials would have carried out their duties watched by crowds of onlookers.

A series of chance discoveries during the last 250 years, and the results of the recent excavations, mean that we can reconstruct the altar in some detail.

Half of it lies within the precinct excavation where it can now be seen.

The altar was a square block of masonry, set on a stone platform, each of its corners being elaborately carved with deities. Three of the four corner blocks survive. One found in 1790 when the Pump Room was built depicts Jupiter on one side, with his eagle standing at his feet, with Hercules Bibax on the adjacent side. Hercules is recognizable because of the lion's pelt cape he wears with its paws knotted across his chest. The second corner, found here in 1965, shows Bacchus with a squatting panther, and a female deity pouring a libation from an upturned jug. The third corner has somehow found its way to the church of Compton Dando, 13 km from Bath, where it can be seen built into an external buttress. It is still possible to make out a finely carved Apollo playing a lyre and a naked male deity possibly Mercury.

Just in front of the altar, still in its original position, is an inscription which says L. MARCIUS MEMOR, HARUSP, D.D. – 'Lucius Marcius Memor, augur, gave this gift' – the gift presumably being a statue, now gone, which originally stood in a recess immediately behind the base.

As augur, Memor would have presided over the sacrifice of sheep, pigs and cattle on the altar paying particular attention to their livers from which he would have been able to foretell the future. He would also have read the omens in flights of birds.

The reconstructed altar and inscribed statue base in situ on the temple precinct.

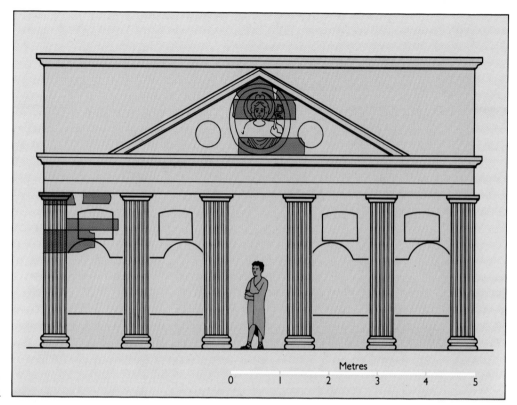

*Reconstruction
of the Facade of
the Four Seasons.*

*Detail of Spring
from the Facade
of the Four
Seasons.*

The Luna pediment.

The Facade of the Four Seasons

Excavations within the precinct over the last 250 years or so have uncovered very many sculptured stones from the various buildings which adorned the temple enclosure. One of these buildings, which we call the Facade of the Four Seasons, can be pieced together in some detail. It very probably stood on the north side of the altar and faced south.

Though carved as a single facade the impression which the original Roman designer was trying to give was of two planes, a row of six fluted columns, with an elaborately ornamented wall behind. This explains why the two are not exactly symmetrical.

The wall between the pilasters was decorated with four rectangular panels, each containing a winged cupid representing a season, set above more elaborated niches in which were four seated figures, probably deities. Very few fragments from the lower row survive but the cupids are well represented among the remaining pieces. Each holds the attribute of his season: Spring, flowers; Summer, corn; Autumn, fruit; and Winter, a bill hook for cutting firewood.

The Facade with its engaged columns is evidently only part of a larger monument which very probably had an attic storey containing a triangular pediment. Reconstructing it in this way gives an altogether more satisfactory appearance and there survive several fragments of a pediment which very probably comes from this building. In the centre is a circular panel depicting the head of Luna, goddess of the night, with the crescent moon around her. In her right hand she would have held the reins of the horses pulling her four-horse chariot across the night sky, while in her left she holds a riding whip.

If we are correct in supposing that this building stood on the north side of the altar looking south, then it would neatly have balanced the monumental doorway (quadrifrons) leading to the spring not only architecturally but also religiously because there is some evidence to suggest that the pediment above the door was decorated with a carving of the head of Sol – god of the sun. There is a very satisfactory balance in having Sol and Luna facing each other in this way representing the power of Sulis over the universe.

23

The Baths

The great Roman bathing establishment, fed by the curative mineral waters was, and indeed still is, one of the wonders of Roman Britain. Much of it can be seen today six metres below the present street level.

JOHN RONAYNE

The focus of the bathing establishment is the Great Bath – a large rectangular swimming bath, lined with lead. It was always roofed, first with timber and later with a masonry vault, unlike the open situation in which it is now displayed.

The Bath was fed with a constant flow of hot mineral waters led direct from the spring in a lead-lined culvert which still works today. The overflow poured out at the northeast corner through a narrow culvert to join the main outfall drain to the north. The actual level of the water was maintained by a sluice, made of bronze, found in position by the excavators in 1880. Although the sluice has been removed and replaced, the drainage system still functions as it did originally.

To the east of the Great Bath were two smaller swimming baths (the second was later filled in) both fed from the Great Bath.

Less is known about the supply of hot and cold water to the west baths but they all drained into a separate culvert constructed to the south of the baths which in turn flowed to join the other outfalls.

Within the baths a constant flow of water was also provided for washing facilities in the south-west corner of the Great Bath Hall and to feed a fountain set in the centre of the north side of the bath. The slots cut for the pipes can still be seen and one of the lead pipes remains in position (p. 32).

Water flowing into the Great Bath as it did in the Roman period.

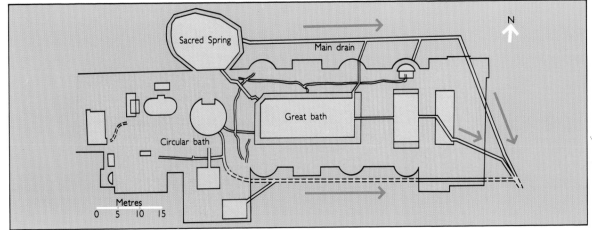

The water supply and drainage system of the baths.

Four stages in the development of the baths.

The bathing establishment underwent a number of renovations and modifications during its 400-year life.

The original arrangement, put up in the 60s and 70s AD was very simple. There were two elements: the thermal swimming baths to the east and a small suite of artificially heated baths to the west. Between them lay a monumental hall (later to contain the circular bath) with magnificent views across the spring to the temple precinct beyond.

Early in the second century AD the west baths were extended while at the east end a completely new set of heated baths were built, replacing one of the earlier swimming baths. This change is particularly interesting because it seems to coincide with an edict passed by the Emperor Hadrian forbidding mixed bathing. Henceforth two separate suites of baths had to be provided, or in the lesser establishments, opening was at different times for men and women.

The third major building period came at the end of the second century or early in the third. By this stage the old roofs were in disrepair. In such a damp atmosphere even massive timbers would have rotted and contorted. The decision was therefore taken to re-roof the hall containing the circular bath, the great bath and the smaller swimming bath beyond, with masonry vaults (see pp. 24–5). It was a considerable undertaking which involved strengthening all the walls and piers, details of which can still be seen.

After this, alterations were on a minor scale until finally, in the fifth century, the old baths were abandoned and a marsh formed.

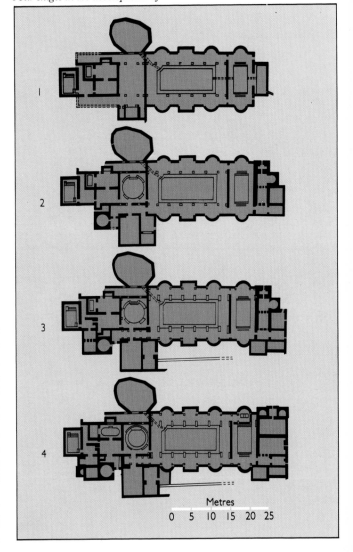

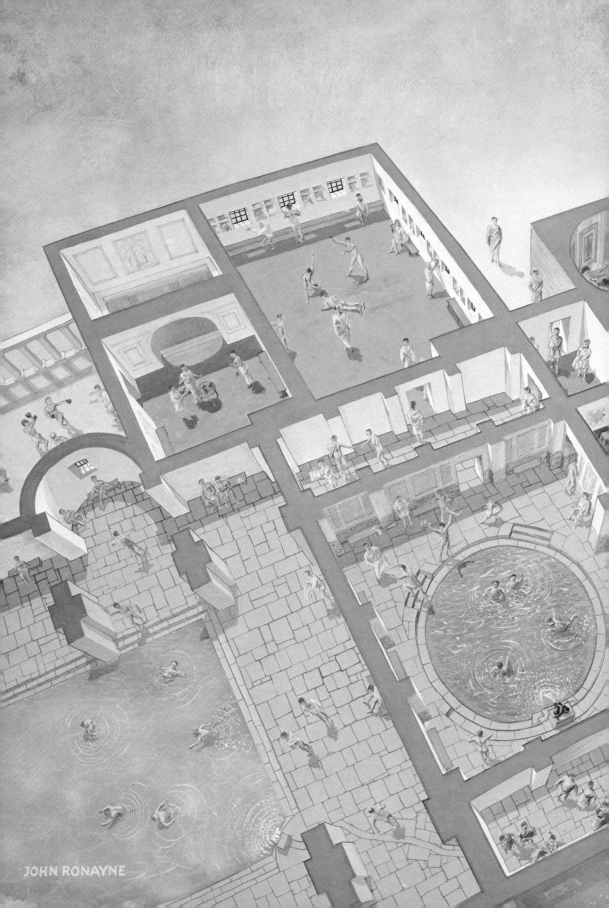

JOHN RONAYNE

THE WEST BATHS in their final form show
just how complicated the Roman bathing ritual
had become with their swimming baths, cold
plunges, saunas and Turkish baths.

Wall flue

Stokehole

Hot baths were essential to a Roman. At their simplest a suite of baths would comprise an undressing room, a cold plunge bath (*frigidarium*), a bath of tepid heat (*tepidarium*) and a hot bath (*caldarium*) together perhaps with an exercise court. More sophisticated establishments like Aquae Sulis also had a room of intense dry heat (*laconicum*) providing a facility very much like a modern sauna.

After taking exercise the bather would first acclimatise himself to the warm heat of the *tepidarium* before making his way to sit and sweat in the *caldarium*. Here he would be oiled and scraped and possibly massaged before finishing his treatment with a quick plunge in the cold bath. Bathing was a social occasion where friends could meet and talk, board games could be played and business transacted.

There would have been entertainers like jugglers present, manicurists, gamblers calling the odds, as well as hosts of servants and slaves running about looking after their masters. Bathing was a noisy, lively occasion essential to an agreeable life.

Bathing began to become popular in Rome in the first century BC and with it went the need to develop an efficient form of central heating. To heat a room, whether for a hot bath or simply to provide ambient heat for a winter living room, the Romans perfected the *hypocaust* – essentially a cavity floor beneath which hot air circulated. Usually, as at Aquae Sulis, the floors were supported on stacks of bricks (*pilae*).

The method of heating was by means of a charcoal-fuelled flue immediately adjacent to the room and it was quite usual to set a large copper boiler above the flue to provide a constant supply of hot water. To draw the hot air into the underfloor chamber it was necessary to create a through draught by means of vertical flues, set in the walls, opening through the roofs. In some cases, when a room needed to be very hot, all the wall surfaces were jacketed with these flue tiles so that no heat would be lost: sometimes even the vaulted roofs were similarly treated.

The thick masonry of the walls, floors and vaults of these hypocaust rooms ensured that once the temperature had been raised the room would remain hot for a long time – the same principle as the modern night storage heater.

The hypocaust from the tepidarium of the west baths. Inset shows circulation of hot air.

Lead water pipe serving the fountain in the Great Bath.

The Plumbers

The efficiency of the baths depended to a large extent on the quality of the plumbing. We have already seen (pp. 26–27) how the overall circulation of water was planned. This would have needed a detailed knowledge of volume and rate of flow, together of course, with the skill to control all the building levels with great accuracy. This level of planning was in the hands of engineers, most probably seconded from the army for the purpose.

All the lead pipes in the baths were made by hand.

Several examples of the plumbers' work survive in the baths. Most impressive is the length of lead pipe still *in situ* in a slot cut in the floor on the north side of the Great Bath. Unlike our modern lead pipes, the Roman pipes were made from a strip of lead, hammered around a pole, so that the edges would touch. The plumber then had to cast a sealing strip of lead along the joint by sticking fillets of clay on either side of the join and pouring molten lead into the gap. To create a properly fused and sealed join needed considerable skill. The separate lengths of pipe were joined in a similar manner.

In addition to making the pipes the plumbers also had to line the baths with lead, not so much to keep water from leaking out but to prevent polluted ground water from seeping into the baths. Much of the lead lining has been removed, but in the Great Bath the original lead sheets still remain in position, in all some 42 sheets weighing $8\frac{1}{2}$ tons. An excavation beneath the paving just to the west of the bath showed that the plumbers worked here before the paving was laid, trimming the sheets and preparing offcuts to melt down for fusing the joints.

Roofing the Baths

In the baths and the temple we see Roman engineering at its best. The foundation work is, for the most part, sound, the hydraulic engineering is very advanced; and the engineers have demonstrated their ability at creating huge vaulted spaces using only the simplest of materials – brick and concrete.

We know most about the vault covering the Sacred Spring because when it fell, in the post-Roman period, substantial parts of it buried themselves in the silt and mud, filling the reservoir and remaining there undisturbed until the excavation of 1979–80.

As soon as the reservoir wall had been completed the entire chamber would have been fitted with a mass of timber formwork, supported on scaffolding, to create a curve representing the underside of the vault. On this, and springing from the wall top, the masons built ribs of brick about 1.5 metres apart joining them at the top to a spine of stone voussoir blocks.

Once the ribs had been completed the space between could be filled. For much of the vault, to reduce the weight, the masons used hollow box-tiles but lower down, on the haunches of the vault where greater solidity was required, a much denser mix of limestone blocks set in concrete was employed in a thickened mass hidden by a vertical wall (as in the diagram). This was designed to convert part of the lateral force of the vault into a more stable vertical thrust.

When the mortar of the vault had hardened the carpenters would have removed the formwork – a tense time until it became clear that the vault was a successful structure! The last act involved the rendering of the vault inside and out with a thick layer of red waterproof mortar. It is unlikely that tiles or roof slabs were used since few have been found in the excavation and anyway such a cladding would have been unnecessary.

One of the problems posed by the roofing of the baths was how to cope with steam and condensation. This was overcome by leaving the ends of the vaults open (though perhaps with a few vertical supports) in much the same way as our railway architects dealt with a similar problem in the nineteenth century. Part of one of these great lunette openings can be seen at the west end of the Great Bath (picture this page).

The face of the vault once roofing the Great Bath.

Section of the vault covering the Sacred Spring.

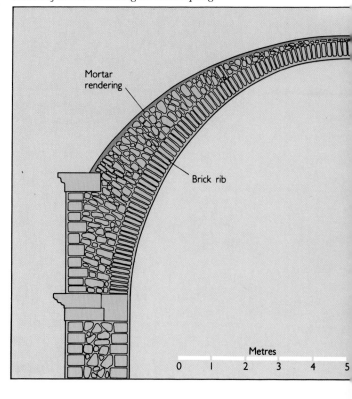

Mortar rendering

Brick rib

Metres

0 1 2 3 4 5

33

Altar set up by a sculptor called Sulinus to the Sulevii (probably a triad of local goddesses).

The City

The little town of Aquae Sulis flourished in the shadow of this great religious complex. Fine houses floored with mosaics sprang up and pilgrims flocked to the Sacred Spring.

Mosaic found in the north-west corner of the town.

Items of everyday life from the Roman town.

Comparatively little is known of Roman Bath outside of the religious complex but excavations over the years have brought to light traces of masonry-built houses and a number of fine polychrome mosaics showing that the inhabitants enjoyed a degree of prosperity.

Dedicatory inscriptions and tombstones give us the names and origins of many of them – Sulinus the sculptor probably came from Cirencester to buy good Bath stone, Priscus a stone-worker (*lapidarius*) came from near Chartres in France. Other foreign visitors included Peregrinus Secundus from Trier and Rusonia Aventina from Metz.

Inside its town wall Bath would have been a crowded place with probably more than half the enclosure given over to great public buildings. Outside, particularly to the north of the walled area along the Fosseway, lay a considerable urban sprawl apparently undefended. One excavation in this area, just outside the wall, exposed a pit full of shoes and leather offcuts.

Certainly by the second century when Bath was at the peak of its prosperity, it would have been a thriving market centre – the focus of a rich and productive countryside – but always it was overshadowed by the presence of the temple.

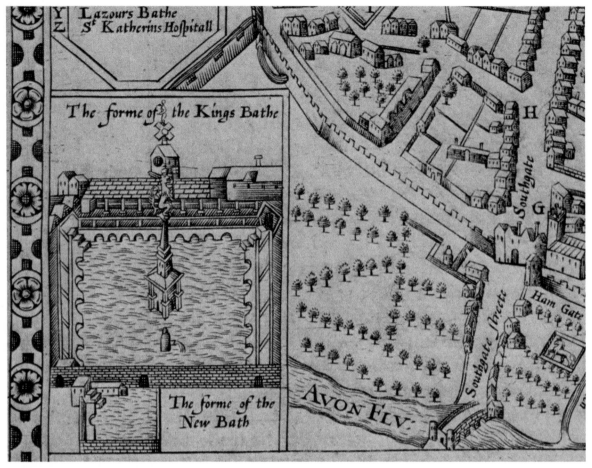

The forme of the Kings Bathe

The forme of the
New Bath

AVON FLV:

Southgate Streete

Southgate

Ham Gate

H

G

Detail from Speed's map of 1610 showing The King's Bath. Below: plan of
the medieval bath set within the old Roman reservoir.

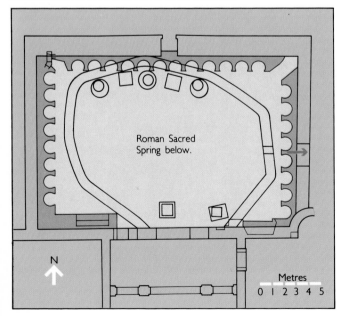

Roman Sacred
Spring below.

N

Metres

0 1 2 3 4 5

After the Romans

Even though the Roman buildings fell into disrepair during the fifth century AD and many of them began to collapse or were used as quarries for building stone, the skeleton of the old Roman town remained dominant; its walls became the medieval city walls, while its three springs continued to flow into the reservoirs which the Romans had built.

The main spring, enclosed within the great vaulted chamber, soon became clogged with sand and after a while the vaulted roof fell in; but still the water bubbled up finding its way through the ruins of the Roman baths to the river. The thick outer enclosure wall remained standing, and although the upper levels were robbed for building stone the lower part was intact and visible in the early Middle Ages. So massive and durable was it that when, in the early twelfth century, the

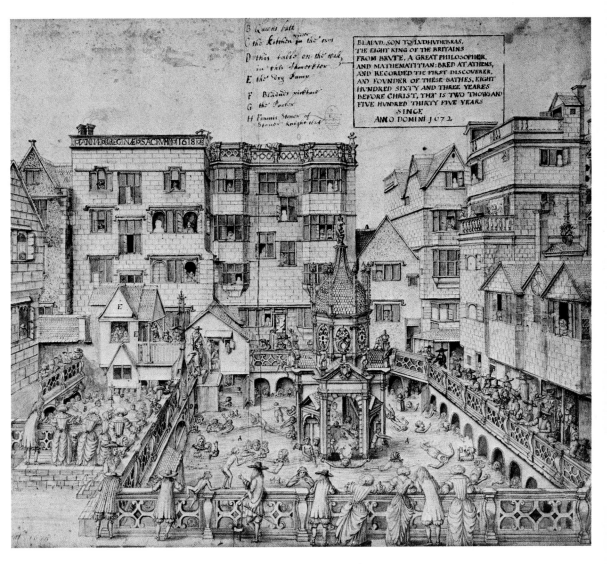

The following labels appear within the drawing:

B Queens bath
C the kitchen in the 1601
D this falle on the wall in this shuverfier
E the Dry pump
F Blenduis picture
G the Baston
H Francis Stoner of Stoner Knight 1624

GANNI REGINÆ SACRVM 1618

BLAUD, SON TO LVDHVDEBRAS,
THE EIGHT KING OF THE BRITAINS
FROM BRVTE, A GREAT PHILOSOPHER,
AND MATHEMATITIAN: BRED AT ATHENS,
AND RECORDED THE FIRST DISCOVERER,
AND FOVNDER OF THESE BATHES, EIGHT
HVNDRED SIXTY AND THREE YEARES
BEFORE CHRIST, THA' IS TWO THOWSAND
FIVE HVNDRED THIRTY FIVE YEARS
SINCE
ANNO DOMINI 1672.

monks of Bath decided to refurbish the spring as a bath – the King's Bath – they used the Roman wall, building niches against its inner face for the bathers to shelter in. These niches were clearly shown, still in use, on Speed's map of Bath and Johnson's drawing.

Throughout the medieval period most of Bath sheltered within its city walls but there were suburbs spreading to north and south. It was much the same size as its Roman predecessor and like the Roman town was dominated by its religious buildings, the great medieval abbey, which occupied so much of the walled area. Medieval Bath was a small but prosperous town depending for its livelihood largely on the production of woollen cloth, but with the decline of the wool industry in the fifteenth and sixteenth centuries so the fortunes of Bath wasted and even the planned rebuilding of the abbey on a much reduced scale had to be abandoned with the work unfinished.

The baths, however, continued to be visited and from the beginning of the seventeenth century began to attract royal and aristocratic families intent on taking the cure. In their wake others followed until by the 1720s Bath was fast on the way to becoming a highly fashionable spa. The sudden rise in the town's popularity meant that improved facilities had to be provided for its visitors.

The rediscovery of the Roman city was the direct result of this large-scale rebuilding in the eighteenth century.

The King's Bath by Thomas Johnson 1672.

Demolition of the Queen's Bath around 1880. The Roman circular bath was discovered underneath.

Discovery

Chance discoveries of the eighteenth century showed that much of Roman Bath remained to be discovered six metres below the streets. But it was not until the Pump Room was rebuilt in 1790 that the first significant traces of Roman public buildings came to light with the uncovering of the temple steps and substantial parts of the highly ornamented temple front. The rediscovery of Roman Bath had begun.

Although the archaeological world took a great interest in the remarkable finds of 1790 no attempt was made to follow up the discoveries for nearly 80 years. In 1867 work began on the demolition of the old White Hart Hotel (opposite the Pump Room on the west side of Stall Street) prior to its replacement by the monumental Grand Pump Room Hotel (itself demolished in 1959). A local amateur archaeologist James Irvine kept a very close eye on the building work and was able to record substantial remains of the temple of Sulis Minerva.

Irvine's work inspired a new interest in the archaeology of Bath – an interest avidly pursued by the City Engineer Major C.E. Davis. Irvine had found part of the outfall drain which Davis, as an engineer, took a particular interest in since he was responsible for overseeing the city's springs. In following the Roman drain, Davis was led towards the King's Bath and realized that the Roman spring head probably lay beneath the medieval structure. His curiosity got the better of him and under the pretence of looking for leaks he ripped up the old floor and began to excavate the Roman reservoir beneath. This work in the spring marked the beginning of a major programme of excava-

tion which was to last, on and off, for about 20 years during which time virtually the entire Roman bathing establishment was uncovered. By the turn of the century Bath could boast a Roman monument unparalleled in north-western Europe.

There matters rested until the 1950s when rebuilding work in the city began again in earnest, for the deep foundations of modern buildings were destroying more and more of the unique archaeological remains. As a response to this increasing threat a new organisation, the Bath Excavation Committee (later to become the Bath Archaeological Trust), was set up to look after the archaeology of the city. After some preliminary trial excavations in the 1960s the Trust, in close collaboration with the City authorities, undertook an extensive excavation in the Sacred Spring and beneath the Pump Room. The work was completed at Easter 1983 when the newly exposed remains – consisting of much of the temple precinct – were opened up as an extension to the museum.

The excavation has immeasurably increased our understanding of one of the greatest monuments of Roman Britain, but it is only a small step towards writing the story of Roman Bath – Aquae Sulis – and its people.

THERE STOOD ARCADES OF STONE THE STREAM HOTLY ISSUED WITH EDDIES WIDENING UP TO THE WALL ENCIRCLING ALL THE BRIGHT BOSOMED POOL THERE THE BATHS WERE HOT WITH INWARD HEAT NATURE'S BOUNTY THAT SO THEY CAUSED TO FLOW INTO A SEA OF STONES THE HOT STREAMS

Extract from a Saxon poem of the eighth century

Bath Archaeological Trust is a charitable trust formed to promote excavations and research into the Roman and later Medieval city. The proceeds of this guide will be used to help finance further archaeological investigations in Bath.

This guidebook has been produced with assistance from Imperial Tobacco Limited.

Back cover: Theatrical mask, probably from a tomb. Findspot unknown

Published by Bath Archaeological Trust 4 Circus Bath
ISBN 0 9506180 12
© Bath Archaeological Trust 1985
Text by Professor Cunliffe
Design and illustration by Threes Company, Oxford
Photography by Fotek, Bath
Perspective illustrations by John Ronayne
Phototypeset by Tradespools, Frome
Printed by Clare, Son and Co, Wells
P37 Johnson Drawing reproduced by courtesy of the Trustees
of the British Museum